First published in Great Britain in 2000 by
POETRY NOW
Remus House,
Coltsfoot Drive,
Woodston,
Peterborough, PE2 9JX
Telephone (01733) 898101
Fax (01733) 313524

HB ISBN 0 75430 955 X
SB ISBN 0 75430 956 8

CATCH THE MOMENT

Edited by

Zoë Rock

FOREWORD

Although we are a nation of poets we are accused of not reading poetry, or buying poetry books. After many years of listening to the incessant gripes of poetry publishers, I can only assume that the books they publish, in general, are books that most people do not want to read.

Poetry should not be obscure, introverted, and as cryptic as a crossword puzzle: it is the poet's duty to reach out and embrace the world.

The world owes the poet nothing and we should not be expected to dig and delve into a rambling discourse searching for some inner meaning.

The reason we write poetry (and almost all of us do) is because we want to communicate: an ideal; an idea; or a specific feeling. Poetry is as essential in communication, as a letter; a radio; a telephone, and the main criterion for selecting the poems in this anthology is very simple: they communicate.

CONTENTS

WATCHING YOU SLEEP

In the treacle heat of this summer's night,
your snowflake face burns white
through layers of dreaming.

All my life I have watched you sleep.
I lay my finger to your cheek -
you are still breathing,

your essence pure and deep
like night-prised blooms whose perfumes seep
into the dark waters of morning.

Deborah Grasshoff

SNOWBOUND

Flakes of ice crystals
In a flurry of whiteness
To young hearts bringing great joy,
Snowballs and snowmen
Toboggans and sleighs
The dream of each girl and boy.

Slipping and sliding
Amid raucous laughter
In pleasure winter can bring,
Old Mister Frosty
Once more reborn
Shows he can do anything.

With black eyes of coal
And red button nose
He joins in all of the fun,
Hoping each moment
Of the day long
Clouds will blot out the sun.

At ending of day
He stands all alone
While sand is sprinkled in eyes,
Then with the dawn
His heart all aglow
He awakens to new joyous cries.

Soon close beside him
Arises a mate
A snowgirl with long carrot nose
And the children all wait
To see if he will
Bend on one knee and propose.

Through frosted window
I gaze in awe
To their dreams I'd never aspire,
I'll just cuddle up
Snug, dry and warm
Next to my blazing log fire.

Len Fox

So Near . . .

The grapes, the grapes . . . sheer perfection -
did not pander to a lush!
Voluptuous, cascading,
bloom emulating young girl's blush.

A master's hand, well instructed,
dipped its brush in morning dew;
moved on then to finish Wedgwood bowl
and other features, two.

Two plump, ripe, sun-kissed peaches,
threatening to soak their skins:
juicy accomplices,
tempting gluttony's sin.

But I can only look and wonder,
at brush-stroke's mastery,
can only gaze and lust and dribble
and remain so hung-ery!

Joy Lennick

THE CUP THAT CHEERS

When modern life its tension brings
And I need to relax a while
I turn my thoughts to favourite things
And soon find that elusive smile.

My teddy in his little chair
With red bow tie and sweater, blue
A spider's web; her lacy lair
Spangled with early morning dew
The gentle rustling of the breeze
That flirts with slender silver birch
Crisp cracker topped with crumbly cheese
A stained glass window in a church
Bright rainbow, arching 'cross the sky
Anchored by angels at each end
A dark suit on a handsome guy
And Christmas cards from far-off friends
Warm firelight's glow on winter nights
When howling wind is locked without
The cheer of coloured Christmas lights
Adorning windows round about.

Within my life so many things
Can bring me cheer, these are a few
And with them hope eternal springs
But failing that, I make a brew!

Kay Spurr

THE GATE STANDS OPEN . . .
FOR US TO PASS THROUGH INTO THE FUTURE

You served us well
proud Bagnall guards of history,
noble and strong -
the grandeur of our chestnut trees
upon the green,
companion sycamore is there -
in summer's heat
their welcome shade and coolness share . . .

Time ambles on . . .
we villagers of old and new
fair saplings bless
of English oak: sturdy and true!
Throughout their lives
another thousand years will roll -
our Sentinels
this future saga will behold!
Each man and beast,
these children of the Earth - their kin -
from stony trough
refreshment find in heat and sun -
a thirsty horse
in gratitude will pause to drink . . .

We Bagnall folk
stand solemn . . . pensive . . . witnessing
our History:
momentous, as the old Earth turns . . .
New Century:

While glorious beacons blaze and burn . . .
Announce the future World
that is yet to come:
In expectation

Hail the new Millennium!

Carolyn Smith

BITTER BREW

Tuning in this morning to the visual affront
That pours from my TV in honeyed voices
Stringing bloodied events
With well practised consonants and vowels,
Distancing his emotions from the text
The anchorman's stony eyes follow me around.

In my small space there's a world stage
More vast than a colosseum,
Broken bodies and spirit, a race in fear.
The silence is horrendous.
Mosquitoes - blood-slaked.
Slaked - quaff on baby tears.
It's news, it's news, it has rhythmic blues,

Measuring minutes in segments between
Aerobics, Weetabix and trendy Reebok shoes . . .
'Til they defile my home again with
Bloodstained guns. Yet I sit dumb.
Gazing into a cup of acrid coffee
That can't be sweetened with tears,

Gulping, as the darkness I ingest,
While the greedy for power and
Psychopaths twin, staining my being
The colour of sin.

Marion Cummiskey

THE LOG FIRE

The flames twirl around seductively,
Whispering 'Do come, come closer to me.'
Deliciously sensual licking the wood,
Enjoying the taste of the burning food.

The heat tempts our bodies to relax and stay
To lounge in armchairs at the end of the day.
Our naked feet sprawl on the grate by the fire,
Our warm toasted frames now filled with desire.

A man and a woman both stretching out,
By the glow of bright flames darting about.
The cold icy air shut away for the night,
A cosy log fire - our winter's delight!

L Hurdwell

THE BLUE CUT BLUES

On rainy days in the firelight glow
Harmonious seeds in me he'd sow
Old sap that rose through his bright eyes spilled
Into my firelit theatre, joyful music filled.
Whilst I sat cross legged on a warm pegged rug
From bellowed cheeks his hits he'd plug
As the ash-pan caught the remains
Of hypnotic dreams from its blackleaded range.
Whenever I into a deep fire stare
He still sits before me in his fireside chair
His bad leg straight and good one bent
As he warms his seat for the cat to rent,
His teeth still jangle in their water-filled glass
As they sing beside him when his good foot taps.

Yet I never heard him play the Blues
When fate decided him to choose,
Not once to me did he recall
The day his stint on him did fall.

His eyes when sunken my eyesight sought
How his hollow cheeks for their last breath fought.
The way he died I would never choose
Yet I never heard him play the Blues.

His seat now cold the cat won't use
And where he's gone they don't play the Blues
His broken limbs are once more strong
Where the morning sunshine greets the night shift's songs.

John Grocutt

UN(GRATE)FUL!

Weeks of hewing, sawing, hauling
The woodstacks piled up high
Surely not time to light the fire
Summer seems hardly gone

So put it off a little while
The weather still is kind
And the chimney must be swept
Forgotten in the spring

Blowing, raining, getting colder
There's no choice for it now
Chimney's swept, light sticks and logs
The routine has begun

We love the cheery warming fire
On winter evenings dark
The water's hot, radiators too.
No need to seek the gym
For to feed its jumbo appetite
One's jumping up and down
And with care it must be stoked
Or it sulks and dies

Used to its ways we'll stay content
Despite the morning chores
Clear out ashes, clean the grate
So roll on May when fire's out.

Dorothy Dosson

SENSES

I love the *sound* of Christmas
The children's squeals of joy,
As they open up their presents
And find a longed-for toy.

I love the *smell* of Christmas
The turkey, pudding too,
The spicy smell of hot mince pies,
To mention but a few.

I love the *sight* of Christmas
The tree with lights so bright,
Filled with little presents,
Which we'll open Christmas night.

I love the *feel* of Christmas,
Of love, goodwill in store
And hope the new millennium brings
Us peace for evermore.

Pat Eves

WINTER WARMTH

Red of berry, red of fire,
Glowing warmth of candlelight,
Comfort of a cosy chair,
Tucked up safely for the night.

Crackling logs and spitting coal,
Nuts a'roasting in the hearth,
Snuggling in a feather bed,
Wallowing in a sizzling bath.

Munching muffins, pancakes too,
Reading tales of deepest lore,
Shadows dancing on the walls
From the lamp behind the door.

Watching faces in the fire
In the glowing embered coals,
Dreaming of another life
Of highest hopes and greatest goals.

Winter is a lovely time
To reflect and plan anew
For the coming year ahead
And how to make your dreams come true.

Mollie D Earl

WITHIN THE SERPENT'S EYE

I watch,

The nicotine stained organza of evening as it casts its wreaths
on the body of the dying light,
The hip sweet, detail dissolving stench of inevitable evening,
as it sucks the juice from my sight,
The darkling oppression as it steals, touching close,
to gulp the air and drown my lungs in fluid night.
I watch . . . it watches . . . it knows I am alone.

I listen,

For my black wing'ed serpent of solitude to come, acreep,
among my half mad, half imagined fears,
For its rise, quick, on silent wings; a liquid living shadow
among the suffocating gloom it nears,
For unseen fangs, afleck with anticipation,
glist'ning in a wetly voracious maw like quicksilver tears.
I listen . . . it listens . . . it knows I am alone.

I feel,

As the loathsome hell worm strikes, black, savage,
throwing living coils, ice cold, about my soul,
As it feeds, gluttonous, swallowing the black, gnawing rats
of my half imagined miseries whole,
As they flee, squealing half shadows on the edge of vision
among the rot and debris of my self control.
I feel . . . it feels . . . it knows I am alone.

I smell,

Its suffocating scent, of raw loneliness as it throws acrid tendrils
into the dank recesses of my mind,
Its hot musk of companionship, a lost memory,
tearing at the muscles of my aching heart confined,

Its well meant, hot razors of perfume; as they make me crave again
those sweet aromas left behind.
I smell . . . it smells . . . it knows I am alone.

I taste,

The sweet, cloying warmth of this terrifying darkening
which hangs on my tongue like honeydew spit,
The hell hot, scalpel tart light of once benign possession
as it curdles, rank, in the throat it once slit,
The faint remembered tang of constant companionship
burning livid sears into the tongue it once bit.
I taste . . . it tastes . . . it knows I am alone.

I know,

This darkness, so ask not to take it from me; for it is me
and I am it and without it I will surely die,
This torch you would light that I may bathe in its glow;
but do not bring it close, for its flames lie,
This bitter freedom conveyed in solitude
and what liberty reclines therein . . . within the serpent's eye!
I know . . . it knows . . . we know we are alone!

Sullivan

GREEK REFLECTIONS

Balmy nights and melting days,
Silver sand, sun's piercing rays,
Brilliant stars and velvet skies,
Surrender to the warm sunrise.

Exotic smells and sun-tan oil,
Leather sandals, foreign soil,
Midnight bathing, old bazaar,
Cruise ships bound for places far.

Photographs and buying gifts,
Through the toes sand gently sifts,
Holidays are made of these,
Golden beaches, tepid seas.

Like liquid wax within a fire,
Depression melts and thoughts soar higher,
Looking back to warmer times,
To warmer people, warmer climes.

Jennifer D Wootton

EVENING LIGHT

Soft click of the latch as I creep out in the evening gloom
Quick flicker of the dancing bats before the autumn moon

Tree branches edge the sky, their secret creatures wait
Staring eyes and talons grip, hoot and quiver calls to make

Farm lights pierce the growing darkness as a chill fills the air
Your hard day is over, time to relax in the fireside chair

Turning quickly to the cottage with its warming light
I enter the cosy room leaving creatures of the night

Wood is burning brightly in the stone fireplace built long ago
Black solid stove of iron sends out its orange glow

Stairs creak as I ascend to look out on the night once more
The moon reflecting in rippling water and shining white on earth's floor

The logs are black and ashes grey, sleep beckons my tired limbs
Comfort taken from my bed until another day begins.

Poppy Ashfield

AN INTERNAL CLINICAL MIRACLE

The cells meet, shake hands and enjoin
To form the pipette fruits of the groin.
The fruit, protected by the warm internal sea
Grows, nauseating the carrier for a short while
As hormones increase and settle into a new style.
New dresses acquired to drape the secret quay.

The cells now shaping into a first faint flutter
Stretch and start to form the human clutter
So well known as you and me.
A heart beats and new blood circulates.
The once forlorn couple, celebrate
The prospect of hopes bouncing on a knee

A body growing with nails on fingers and toes
Hair in place and the carrier positively glows
As old fashion knitting starts.
Like an astronaut in space swimming weightless
Depending on its carrier and cord but stateless
Unknown are the paths a new life charts.

The carrier, as usual a triumphant female
Demonstrates again that her gender is far from frail.
She may fancy the odd lump of cheese or coal
But still she works on without a to-do
And plans for a room in pink or blue
But her quick rushing step is down to a stroll.

Growing on, preparing to be a universal centre
When cast away from a warm but worn placenta
Into the strange, muddled, busy world outside
Where the nine month muffled sound becomes noise
Those far off cells now shaped to give long hoped for joys
For loving parents to present with justified pride
A modern miracle.

John Aldred

ARMCHAIR TRAVELLER

The old woman, tied to her chair by pain,
Gazes out at the Midland's rain,
But in her mind's eye she can see the crest,
The mighty towers of Everest.

She sits and stirs in her hard wooden chair
Smelling the damp and the fume-filled air,
But in her ears are the splash and the dip
Of porpoises larking as they follow her ship.

She sits and waits to be put to bed
But the pictures continue the show in her head;
And as she snugs the shawl round her arms
She can feel the swaying of coconut palms.

She stretches her limbs and flexes her back,
Peers at the wallpaper's splintering crack,
But inwardly, as the one bar glows
She is viewing the splendours of eternal snows!

Ruth Parker

IN NEARLY CHRISTMAS WEEKS

The sharpness of cold in each morning's air,
The rising sun's redness in eastward trees,
(Devoid of warmth), prove we're in winter's snare.

All winds have stilled, the air is bound to freeze,
And make sloping ice-rinks of Broughton's lanes.
However harsh winters are, they can't 'Sleety'.

The Humber in an ice-grip. Sleety rain
Practises hard to be snow, but falls short
Of that white mantle children crave - in vain.

Toboggan hung in sheds used to be bought
Of whittled when Christmases had been white . . .
They stay there - in despair of much more sport.

Gillian C Fisher

SNOWBOUND

Winter's here again, frost is on the ground
The crunching of snow, an old familiar sound
Iced windowpane, resembling shattered glass
Snowdrifts on the road, vehicles cannot pass
Media go crazy, focusing on isolated towns
But it's just fluffy snow, lying on the ground
I remember England in nineteen sixty-three
Being four years old, the snow as high as me
Icicles hanging, from the eaves of my roof
Reminding me now, of a frozen sabre tooth
How I revelled, in the magic of those days
Mum running a bath, my temperature to raise
I wish she could see me now, with my little girl
Christmas decorations, garlands we unfurl
Sequential flashing lights, loving every minute
Looking for a snowdrift, jumping straight in it
Some people complain, others take the chance
To frolic in the snow, dance the snowman dance
Appreciate the warmth, the fire's orange glow
After playing with their children, in the fresh winter snow.

Danny Coleman

ON A WARM NIGHT

A winter's breeze, on a dark, cold night.
Wanting warmth, company and light.
Just sit by the fire and watch it burn,
Dancing colours, twist and turn.
Be entranced by the flickering flame.
So violent and deadly but yet so tame.
Feel the yellow, orange and gold.
You'll never know you felt the cold.

Claire Hall (14)

FESTIVITY

Spring lies wrapped in her bodice of Earth,
close covered in a crisp leaf shawl
patiently biding till winter's rage subsides,
making plans of petal feathering.
The joys of winter seem yet to come
only the drab of its middling -
mists slowly across the shortest day,
Earth's very soul in melancholy tethering.
So, we, our cotton frosting create
and, with silken fashioned snow charms scattered
'pon branches rescued from dampened cold,
laden shuttered homes in sparkled comfort, tinselled treat.
Thus winter's early magic claims her time
in church bell's greeting, and candle glow,
as we watch dancing wall shadows,
in flickered warmth, it's drabness deplete,
putting summer smiles on wind-scrubbed faces,
before winter herself, in majesty, transforms
huddled treetops and crouching hedges,
with snowdrape gowns and frosting tresses.
Then rooftops smothered in ice-drip glitter
proudly adorn flame-coddled lives
festooned within, festooned without,
under low sun's laughter, silver moonlight's caresses.

M C Lawrence

WINTER

The bitter wind brings snowflakes o'er the hill,
The cattle herd together in the byre.
The bubbling brook is silent 'neath the ice,
And I'm content to slumber by the fire.

Long is the night and chilly is the morn.
Silent the birds, the flower buds are few.
The smell of buttered toast pervades the air.
Oh to be home 'til spring returns anew.

B Williams

RACONTEUR

I think now of tales you told me,
As we sat, on a winter's night,
So cosy, before the fireplace,
By the hazy, warm, firelight;
I'd heard them time and time again,
But to you they were all anew,
As you recalled your boyhood,
In the town where you lived, and grew;
Your face was such a picture,
In the flickering firelight's glow,
As you told, so animatedly,
The stories of long ago;
You carried out all the actions,
You played out every part,
And I watched in fascination,
As you told it from the heart;
Sometimes I roared with laughter,
Sometimes you made me sad,
But always you enthralled me,
With the tales you told me, Dad;
And now I sit alone here,
In the chill, as the fire burns low,
And I think of those other evenings,
When we sat here, long ago;
And sometimes I feel happy,
But mostly I feel sad,
And my heart aches with such longing,
For the wonderful friendship we had.

Dorothy Neil

SEASONAL JOY

Winter snowflakes
     Here again,
Better this than
     Chilly rain.

Time to bring in
     Christmas cheer,
Snowflakes on this day
     So dear.

Now like a Christmas card
     It will be,
As the heavens watch
     Joyfully.

Nature sings her
     Winter's song,
Another year has
     Come and gone.

Around a fireside
     Friends will meet,
Lovers with their lips
     Will greet.

All in tune with this
     Time of year,
Love, peace, goodwill,
     Good cheer.

At Christmas time
     Let's make amends,
Renewing friendships
     Shaking hands.

To plough our lives
      And be as one,
The day God sent
      His only son.

Martin Caley

THE BUSKER

Standing in a haze of heat and frenzied shoppers,
Not familiar with the passers-by,
He hadn't dared do this before,
But a busker must accept averted eyes.

They weren't to know he'd lost a well-loved job,
Even though he'd worked hard all his life,
If he didn't try to earn some cash,
How could he ever face his family and his wife.

Nervous he picked up his guitar,
And put a small box near his aching feet,
Haunting music filled the air,
Amazed, the people stood enraptured in the crowded street.

Music lifts the soul from deep despair,
Its lilting echoes have a beauty of their own,
And this stranger they had hardly noticed,
Wove a magic that they'd never know.

Elaine Beresford

THE ARSONIST AND HIS PEN-PAL

Send you grey-blue signatures of smoke
Between looping letters our lives meet
Detect the murmur of a heartbeat
Begin repairing what was once broke

Make you a picture out of matches
Of Pudding Lane, 1666
With my great grandad rubbing two sticks
He wasn't mentioned in dispatches

The smoke spells love when I write again
Though you think my 'v's look more like 'u's
It's your irrelevance I value
Let the 'x's of kisses explain

Last in alphabet smoke dialogue
Words form paragraphs of affection
I shape and send in your direction
On our fire of love, another log.

A Stothard

EVENINGTIME

As the evening draws in,
When at last all is hush,
Time to reflect
On a day full of rush.

Look at each moment,
The good and the bad,
What things made you happy
And others so sad.

Bless all the events,
Everything that has been,
Opportunities taken,
Others unseen.

See each day as a whole,
Full and complete,
A beginning, a middle,
An ending replete.

Think of the day,
And thank God above,
For each precious moment
He has given with love.

Barbara Manning

FIRELIGHT FLICKERING

I remember
In December
Firelight flickering
No more bickering
Just playing games
Not calling names
All peace and goodwill
Snow on windowsill
Our cat purring
No wind stirring . . .

Daddy home from work
So no fear did lurk
In heart or mind
We just could find
A new book to read
To fulfil our need
New game to play
To make our day.
Keeping ourselves warm
Instead of a storm.
Some happy days
The Lord be praised!

Pauline M Clarke

MOONLIGHT

I have tried to hold
the magic of a moonlit night
while soft my gentle baby sleeps;
moments of peace and my delight
in all her smiles and cries.
Tried to recall your caring ways,
forgotten the pain of birth-close days;
for broken nights and tired eyes.
To tell you how it feels this bond
and how my life is filled with song
watching the pretty baby-play;
but all the days they wind away
summer flown and once again
I think another moonlit night
sweet times, they are not long.

L A Churchill

WELCOME

Blaze the fire in thy grate
Upon my guest I do await
Food prepared the wine is chilled
A cosy home where winter's stilled
Sweet music fills thy room
Casts out the snowy winter's gloom
My guests arrive and all is well
Around log fire those stories to tell
Of childhood memories from long ago
Forgot the cold the wind and snow

Ann Hathaway

BACKWATER

A lowly marsh of unfettered
bearing passed thro' my eye that summer's day,
and I was bound to this broad
acre it lives within me even now.
My eagerness traced is jagged
rim where endless ripples dallied to and fro,
and my still form quivered before me where lilies grow
contented in their mortal freedom.
Youthful breezes swirled their
scents they dashed full rushes to frenzied motions,
and light beams washed this bounty
water margin shadows sharpened still.
In silence, countless to a whim
excited colours charged my view,
their succulence preened my inner
inventions and I was teased beyond recall.
Freshening rain descended
freely its rawness dulled my mental train,
captured by those unkempt
pastures I watched the stillness return anew.
Root battalions shared my
hour their charms had reaped my every stare,
those wild geese scramble to brake their
anchorage winging the freeways on vanishing cries.
In sleepy pockets of comely
England where honeybees comb the floral enclaves,
carefree hairstreaks roam on bramble
dreaming ever in this fair place.

Tom Griffiths

WINTER WONDERLAND

Where frost's caress has touched with icy hand:
When silently he settled in the night
Upon each twig and branch in pale moonlight,
Now trees become a winter's wonderland.

The grass will shine pearl-white at early dawn:
Dead flowers in the garden will once more
With new bright dazzling garb, seem as before
Harsh winter made them blighted and forlorn.

The early morning sky with darkening cloud
Will bring the snow to blanket nature's scene,
And where frost's handiwork had lately been
The swirling drifts will hide with winter's shroud.

At eventide the sun's red setting glow
Enhances shadows that steal one by one;
To bring the night, now winter's day is done,
And its last dying rays light up the snow.

Jack Judd

WHAT IS POETRY?

Can it be but a medium to give sustenance to inspiration.
Can it be but a stepping-stone, to give vent to one's imagination.
Can it be all of many things, a statement, or a better way to state.
Can it be expression in melodious harmony, or just words, for
words own sake!

Can it be but the use of rhyme and reason to words, that give poetry
a true theme.
Can it be that words, extracted from the imagination, are made to mean
far more than they seem.
Can it be but to express oneself, much better than one ought!
Can it be but a way to give simple expressions, some meaning and
a new rhythm to a thought.

Can it be but just another way, another way to communicate.
Can it be a means to express oneself, or a better way to relate.
Can it be but the use of just a simple way, to use the spoken word.
Can it be that if often is the only way, that one can be really heard!

Can it be but the placing of written words, in the best order of things.
Can it be but the use of inspiration and all that, that word brings.
Can it be but thoughts to paper, when thoughts are apt to stray.
Can it be but a way to make a point, when there's something
worthwhile to say.

Can it be of many things, as a way to have some fun.
Can it also be a way to reminisce, when one's day is nearly done.
Can it be true emotion, formed from life's experiences from afar.
Can it bring a meaning to life itself and to who we really are.

Yes poetry can mean many things and it has many things to give.
But poetry was more than a gift to me, for it gave me a reason to live.

Charlie Walker

Do You Remember?

Do you remember looking up at the sky
Making pictures in the clouds as they passed by.
Saw pictures of what you wanted to do
When the future looked so exciting to you.
Do you remember?

Do you remember your very first kiss
And knew never again would you feel like this.
You were on cloud nine as you walked hand in hand
The only two lovers in the whole of the land.
Do you remember?

Do you remember as a very young bride
When you walked up the aisle at your father's side.
When your family and friends filled the church that day
When you promised to honour, love and obey.
Do you remember?

Do you remember your first baby boy
How he filled your arms with so much love and joy
How you watched your children grow with pride
How they made you laugh but sometimes you cried.
Do you remember.

Now if you stop and look up at the sky
And make pictures in the clouds as they pass by.
Do you remember what you once wanted to do
Or have the pictures gone - just faded from view?
A lifetime to remember.

M Millar

AROUND THE LOG FIRE

Draw up a chair around the log fire,
Enjoy the sheer pleasure,
The sound of crackling,
The warmth of the red and orange glow,
The playful light flickering across the room.

How cosy it is
Just snuggled up by the fire,
Your favourite book on your lap,
A piece of tapestry, knitting or crochet
or whatever you enjoy.

Have your favourite music on in the background
Turn your thoughts to others . . .
Friends, family, people you know.
Plan to see them in the near future,
Pick up the phone and arrange a date.

When it's cold and dark outside
There's no better place to be,
Snuggled up by the old log fire
with a cup of cocoa or tea!

Cathy Mearman

ONCE MORE WE WERE ONE

I'd saved the logs for nights like these,
and as I light the fire
I watch the flickering, dancing flames
as they rise ever higher.

We'd spent so many wintry hours
together, you and I
until death snatched you from my arms
and I was left to cry.

I huddle near, and through my grief
find comfort in its heat,
and sense my love is close, to make
my life once more complete.

Her face smiles through its rich warm glow
and fills my soul with calm
because I know my darling love
lives free and safe from harm.

I'd shivered on the warmest days,
yet now that chill has gone
for she has come to mend my heart
and tell me to go on.

The fire casts shadows round the room
and holds me in its spell.
It crackles, as I hear her voice
soft whisper 'All is well.'

I sit beside the fire until
its work is almost done,
and yet its flame can never die
for once more we are one.

John Christopher

IMAGINATION AND MOONLIGHT

Alone with my imagination,
And moonlight for company,
I walked towards my destination,
In perplexed uncertainty.

I had walked the darkened lane before,
With a more confident stride,
But this was the night when abstruse lore,
Had reasoning on its side.

The lane was full of shadows that night,
With some strange gnarled twisted trees,
That seemed to change shape in the moonlight,
And made me feel ill at ease.

Wondering whatever it might be,
In the corner of my eye,
I could feel the unreal watching me,
Through those peepholes in the sky.

At my feet a layer of stardust,
Like sequins scattered my path,
While just one cloud, like a wanderlust,
Seemed to cut the moon in half.

Its shadow was chased across the ground,
With the moonlight in pursuit,
And my heartbeat was the only sound,
Except for a lone owl hoot.

Unknowing I had quickened my pace,
I was running more or less,
Behind me, terror began to chase,
And I was its prey, helpless.

The more it pursued, the more I fled,
Panic overtook my mind,
Impelled to escape my awesome dread,
Those shadows were left behind.

Chased to the other side of midnight,
And the safety of my lair,
By imagination and moonlight,
And whatever else was there.

Peter Chaney

MAGIC MAN

A white rabbit in a hat,
By his side a tabby cat.
White rabbit in a hat,
Where is the man who sat,
and conjured you from there,
when he placed you upon the chair?

Tabby cat, can you tell me that
you sat so still without a care,
and you didn't even *see a hare?*
the hare that landed over there,
and where's the man?
        The magic man?

He is the one who disappeared,
whilst you sat preening at your beard.

J Merrifield

A WARM GLOW

Central heating is a great boon,
With constant heat all through the house
Instead of one room hot and the rest icy
As it used to be. But something is missing.
There is heat, but not warmth and no focal point
As there is with a good fire, especially a log fire.
I remember cold winter evenings and gathering round
Our fire. The logs shifting, sparks popping out;
Smoke drifting in the flames, fairy tales, mysteries.
The log fires did more than keep us warm. We roasted
Chestnuts; made toast by them - hot and buttered - with
A smoky flavour which no electric toaster will produce.
The fire was a living thing that gave companionship.
It gave not just heat, but a warm glow in our lives.

Pamela Sansom

BALLAD

In the chilly dusk of December
By the light of the frosty moon,
A poor man came to the palace gate
To beg a humble boon.

'Some kindling sticks for my good wife
And a bowl of broth for the bairn -
We'll surely suffer this bitter night
If you cannot give us alms.'

The lady gave him a bundle
And her cheeks were wet with tears.
Her eyes were dim and her hands were cold
In spite of her jewels and furs.

'Oh what can ail you, madam?
You can eat and drink your fill -
You've plenty of wood by your fireside
And a bed to keep out the chill.'

'A bed to keep out the chill, that's sure -
But none to take my hand -
I grieve for the lack of my long-lost lord
Who rides in a far-off land.

'I light the lamp at my window
And nightly prepare a feast
Of fish and fowl in a golden bowl,
With wine of the richest and best.

'But the lamp will gutter to blackness
And the flesh wither off from the bone,
The wine will all be drunken down
Before my lord comes home.

'Take warmth and cheer to your darlings -
My blessings go with my boon!
But let you remember this lonely soul
Who sits by the lonely moon.'

Margaret Ericsen

LOG FIRE VERSE

Blank stare . . .
Why are they so comfortable

Staring into the flames of the fire
Listening to the wooden logs hiss and crackle

Thinking a thousand worlds away
Thinking a thousand miles away

Why does one always end up staring
Into the angry flames of a fire

Thinking what could be and wishing
Thoughts of all and life's desire

A deep silence falls upon your thoughts
Nothing to interrupt but loud cracks in the logs

You end up thinking about all sorts
Different sentences, lines and epilogues

Things come to mind from years ago
Memories you never knew you had

Not even feeling the heat and harsh glow
But somehow thinking usually makes one sad . . .

Glennys Baker

LISTEN

Listen
A bird is singing
As you open your door
To a new morning
Busy with motors
Milk bottles and mail.

Listen
A bird still sings
Beyond the closed door
Beyond the double-glazed
Centrally heated cocoon
Of comfortable warmth.

Listen
This bird's song
Loud and insistent
Is more important
Than all you will do
Think or say today.

Listen
As it sings
Through the mist
Of a cold winter dawn
Sunless and dismal
Still wreathed in grey.

Open the door again
Stand a full minute outside
Until the cold creeps
Right inside your mind

Listen
A bird is singing.

Richard Stewart

SNUGGLE, CRACKLE AND POP

As I entered the dimly-lit room
Most people would frown with gloom,
And moan if they dare
The smell of burning wood filled the air.

As I sat in my chair
Sipped my drink and looked with a glare,
The fire crackled and popped
Of the logs that I've chopped.

The flames flickering and glowing brightly
The fire filled the place bold and mighty,
The warmth, warming me through
My thoughts drifted and began to drew.

There's something about a log fire
Perhaps another log to sort my desire,
As I sat nice and cosy
My cheeks feeling red and rosy.

Steve Wright

PICTURES IN THE FIRE

On winter's night a coal fire
Embers glowing bright
Imagination stirs me
In memory's fleeting flight
Two lovers sitting closely
Beneath an old oak tree
The old bridge, by a mill pond
A heron in a stream

Another log on embers
The pictures changing shape
A smiling face of loved one
An old familiar place
My dreams, a cosy farmhouse
In a peaceful island chase
The flames of fire flicker
As logs begin to hiss
Then spit out sharp hot embers
To break a dream of bliss

Mackintosh

LOG FIRE VERSE

An easterly wind, keen and sharp,
rises and falls: Poised as a
fragile dress of silk
refusing to be anchored.

The garden, transformed,
gleams white.
Wills snow-covered plants
to battle bravely through the earth.

Frosty stars encircle the heavens.
The moon stares cold:
Reflects in pearly light
the icy bosom of the land.

Gales assail the lattice:
A symphony of the spheres
embraced by nature's zephyr,
mingles with the wail of tortured trees

Safe from its rush
I, a cherished sheaf,
recline secure.
Content within your arms.

Whipped by red and orange flames
logs crackle - frivolous!
Clasped against the elements
two shadows pose in stark relief

Fire, cavorts! Sparks! Exposes
the passion displayed within your eyes.
Love bolsters all.
This, is a warm and happy place.

June Crosby Jackson

THE FRIGHTENING TREE

The twisted branches of the frightening tree,
Where bats and ravens secretly reside,
Curl gnarled elbows forming a hide
Away from eyes that strive to see.

The snakish arms of tortured wood
Protect Hob Goblins and Trolls, although
This is a place where Fairies will not go,
For it nurtures evil; never good.

If you discover the frightening tree,
Run away - search your soul within;
Or the crinkled arms will suck you in,
Forever a prisoner - never to be free.

Ted Harrison

ALL IS COSY

Long shadows play daringly on the walls,
While winter wind whistled around the eaves,
But all is cosy in the sitting room.

Sense of calm cossets the house as night falls,
Outside, sounds heard are wind and rustling leaves,
Inside, there's crackling fire, clock chiming boom.

Family playing games, hope no-one calls,
Snugly enclosed, only themselves to please,
Happy together, avoiding night's gloom.

S Mullinger

A WELCOME AWAITING

Lights twinkle in the darkness
Proving living homes are there,
The sky, like pitch, is sombre,
Trees black, gaunt and bare.

A January day is ending,
Pavements glisten in street lights,
People scurry to their dwellings,
Out of darkness into bright.

Raging winter hems life in,
It's a tunnel to be travelled
Before spring days dawn again
Storm clouds must be unravelled.

Yet, some there are who never
Feel the welcome of a room,
Life has brought cold misery,
They're shrouded in the gloom.

Not for them a cosiness waiting,
The sinking comfort of a chair,
A hearty meal straight from the oven,
A family waiting there!

Winter days are banished
From my home on long, chill nights,
Yet, I remember, but for God's grace,
I might be in their plight!

Pat Heppel

CHILDHOOD NIGHTS

Throw another log upon the fire,
draw tight the curtains, shut out the night.
Lower the lights, let shadows creep,
savour the feeling - all is alright.

Set chestnuts popping on the fire -
toasted toes just inches from the blaze -
happy faces, reflected red,
as into the leaping flames they gaze.

Outside, the snowflakes fall and swirl,
and ice-cold winds do roar and howl,
the darkness ever blacker gets,
it is no night for man - or fowl!

Then Mother brings hot chocolate,
and hands the mugs around,
we sip the sweetness - ecstasy!
the crackling logs the only sound.

Then comes the time that I love best -
a tale to tell, to beat the others!
My sister's dreamy, of knights, romance -
no-nonsense ones are Mothers.

I tell of heroes, courageous, bold -
mystery from Father - a *spooky* one!
We listen, shivering in delighted fright -
how glad we are when it is done!

Our nodding heads soon tell on us,
but, of course, we want to stay,
it's *cold* upstairs, though in our beds
we know hot water bottles lay.

Dad sets to with poker, the fire is duly raked,
the ash falls through, leaves flickering glow -
the guard is brought and set in place -
Goodnight, dear fire, burn low.

Joyce Hockley

DREAMING

Sitting by the fire I often wonder why
The flames are red and yellow
Sparks from the burning wood fly high,
The warmth, the peace, tranquillity
I find just gazing mesmerised
Drifting off into oblivion
Then I awake with a sense of surprise
Such a natural hum-drum thing
Sitting by the fire
Next time you gaze into it
Drift away with your desires.

Susan Askew

No Surrender

The pride and the passion;
A martyr by name.
Poor misguided souls;
It ends just the same
In death and destruction;
Or a lifetime in gaol.
They think their cause worthy
But in practice they fail
To alter the system
One iota or jot:
But the world's terrorists
Are a cold-blooded lot.
Their methods are madness;
They never must win:
To bow to their terror,
Destruction and sin
Would be madness itself.
The law will stand firm
In defence of democracy.
Will they never learn?

Graham P Manuell

FUEL FOR THOUGHT

The infinitesimal spark of flame
alleviated blue shadow tones'
sepulchral gloom,
a separateness one could not name,
framework to half-closed eyes and old bones
eased in warm room.

Somehow an affinity between
vermilion and vibrant glows
of firelight niche
and long ago, nostalgic scene,
those intertwining dreams exposed,
a-dazzle rich.

'Remember waltzing?' someone sighed;
'Those fascinating gentle treads
on spindly heel?
Can you recall the Palais Glide,
skirts a riot of blues and reds
of wild appeal?'

Whilst they watched smoke lilac spirals glance
as evasive, sweet as reverie
there was revived
the charm and the mystery of dance.
'Think of how we jitterbugged till three
and how we jived!'

'Husbands, heroes, lover boys have gone;
within their arms how enthralled we swung,
the band a gem.'
One bent to put another log upon
the blaze; mesmerised, they drowsed among
what induced them

back to the ballroom, back to war,
kaleidoscopic cares and joys
and rhythms' trill
like magic thing about a floor
where music smitten girls and boys
were dancing still.

Ruth Daviat

THE 6.03 INTERCITY EXPRESS

Last goodbyes, some unsaid,
loved ones, left still in bed.
Silently out of the door,
ironically, to use no more.

6.03 Intercity Express,
speeding along under duress.
Mangled, metallic mess,
overturned motionless.

Silent now mobile phone,
ownership is not known.
Briefcase locked for ever,
it's secrets told never.

Cherished daughter and son,
now dead spared are none.
Loving husband or wife,
abruptly robbed of life.

Family and friends mourn,
relationships torn.
Tears on their face,
flowers left in place.

Let there be shame,
On those to blame.
So many lives lost
And why? To cut cost.

Sue M Duckworth

WHAT IS HAPPENING TO ENGLAND?

There's money for the criminals who maim and rob and kill,
But little for the aged when they are feeling ill.
The ones who've paid their taxes and never asked for care,
Are told when needing treatment, there is no bed to spare.

There's money for the Millennium Dome, and a wheel
                                    that won't go round,
But money for the NHS? - There's none that can be found.
There's cash for compensation, large payouts are not rare,
But more for education? There's no extra money there.

More cash for N H care beds, more money to retire?
These are just non starters, like the Thames River of Fire.
More money for the farmers? - Well it does not make us laugh,
When at the cattle market they get 1p for a calf.

Most fruit is now imported, while our orchards rot and fade,
But according to the Government this is called free trade.
The pounds have changed to kilos, and although we may sound clever,
Two kilos' worth of Brussel Sprouts will nearly last forever!

The victims are the guilty, and the guilty are reprieved,
How much longer does New Labour think that we will be deceived?
If I could have a penny for every lie they've told,
I'd return it to the country to replace the 'sold off' gold!

Janet Jones

BEYOND FORGETTING

I switched on the television.
The pictures were harrowing and haunting.
Hundreds of people were walking;
Walking along dirt tracks,
Fleeing from persecution,
Possessing little but the clothing on their backs,
The sun relentlessly burned down.
There was scant shelter, food or water
But they were driven on by fear of slaughter.
Desperately they sought safe haven,
To know that they were not forsaken.
Away from their homeland they set up camp,
In appalling conditions where diseases were rife.
Children, lost or orphaned, wandered around and pitifully cried,
Daily the frail and the old people died.
Even there they were threatened by genocide.
Such acts of atrocity occur world-wide.
Will people ever try to put their differences aside?
Pray that all will see the futility of strife,
Come to value all life,
And learn to live together in peace and harmony.

Dorothy Springate

THE LONDON EYE

Riding the London Eye,
wider and ever wider grows my world,
and ever further my horizons stretch.
How like to life. My childhood's narrow world
has widened as each passing year has brought
new scenes, new friends, new interests, new thoughts.

Riding the London Eye, one cannot stop.
As I descend, that wide horizon shrinks;
And more constricted, smaller, grows my world.
Will this, too, be my life as I grow old?

John Lord

CHRISTMAS PAST

Settles the dust of driven snow,
   icing shoulders, mantled white;
powdered breath and cornflake steps
   hushed beneath the tangerine light,
   on the edge of dark, periphery of night.
Of ice-ridged panes I stare
   at a picture card mind's eye view;
of Victorian perfect Christmas
with sugared plums and angel wings,
   firs green with envy, geese that flew
   in midnight skies of cobalt blue.
Half-smiled, I shed these tears
   at all the ghosts of Christmas past
remembering how things used to be
and how they may never be the same
   for the seal is set, the die is cast,
   and I miss you so much, both first and last.

Tony Bush

WINTER TALES

As we sit, the firelight flickers.
Friendly shadows on the wall
Whisper softly autumn's over,
Summer is beyond recall.
Snowy mantles soon will cover
Every inch of brown and green.
Jaunty robin will delight us
Whenever he comes on the scene.
Winter chill may wreak much havoc
With icy roads and blustery gales
Yet long, dark nights we'll fill with pleasure
As we recount our winter tales.

Rosemary Thomson

FOR MY FRIENDS

Like a dazzling star
That sparkles in the night
Like a precious diamond
With facets clear and bright
Like a bright new dawn
Bringing new promising light
Or a glorious sunset
Scarlet blazes bring delight
True, lasting friendship
Can compare to all these things
I'm so glad you're my friend
With all the magic friendship brings.

Elizabeth Loy

THE BRIGHTEST LITTLE BUTTON

Her name is Charley Harris, and she's only five years old,
She suffered meningitis, and blood poisoning took hold,
They amputated both her legs to save her little life,
They gave her artificial limbs and Charley stood no strife,
It should have been about three months before she got the knack,
But Charley wasn't going to hang about as long as that.
In just a couple of weeks she stood up on her plastic plates,
She wanted to get back to school and play with all her mates,
In no time, she was walking, this courageous little girl,
She's the brightest little button in the world!

Mick Nash

HELEN
(In Memory Of Helen Rollason)

Halos of love surround you just now,
With all pain and sadness wiped from your brow.
Such a beautiful smile, and heart dusted gold,
We now feel your happiness with memories to hold.

A legacy of love was left here by you,
Fresh as the morning beaded with dew.
Your daughter so loved, will share all your dreams,
With good wishes blown down on shining moonbeams.

An example to every one who crossed your path,
Giving others a purpose and a reason to laugh.
You dealt with each day with a courage laid bare,
Finding hope sent on rainbows, for people everywhere.

Now you're in a garden, with its beauty just to see,
Walking with the angels, and at peace for eternity.
It was a pleasure just to see you, and share some of your days.
We have reason to be thankful, in so many ways.

Janice Thorogood

IT DOESN'T REALLY MATTER ANYMORE . . .

Death, destruction, famine, greed and war
Hard hitting headlines that don't hit *home* anymore
Our hearts hardened to all that was once wrong
We've seen too much, it's all been around too long
Images that would have once reduced us to tears
No longer register, we don't see, feel or hear
I, me, self is all that seems to matter
Who cares if the rest of the world is in tatters
The media's reporting of all things gone wrong
Has hardened our hearts, all of our compassion has gone.

J Gatenby

PEACE!

Do you think there ever will be peace?
Will the bloodshed ever cease?
Harmony is just one little word,
If we shout it loud enough will it be heard?

Or has the worst just begun?
With both sides shouting, 'Yes we've won'
Cause every day ends just the same
With people dying, people getting maimed.

Every day is full of hideous crimes,
Please, listen this one last time.
Let there be peace, let harmony flow,
Give up these wars, let the hatred go.

Let there be peace.

Mark Brown

BLACK LIST

Black,
the silence gathers in corners
stopping our words
darkening our minds
eclipsing the sun.

Silently fearful
we close up our shutters
pull down the night
bury our heads.

Beneath the bed are whispers -
'Are you now
or have you ever been . . .?'
Names upon names,
some that we've heard
some we'll never know.

We lay silent waiting for light
for the sunrise,
some illumination,
hoping that will come before the knock,
though we know
that with the dawn
we will be a little less.
It is the silence that kills.

Pam Redmond

ENJOY IT WHILST YOU'VE GOT IT

Enjoy it whilst you've got it
Spend it as you may,
For there are those among us
Who'll take it all away.

They'll wait until you're sick,
Fragile and all alone
'You can't stay here, they'll blithely say
'You *must* go in a home.'

Of course, you'll have to sell your house
To pay the nursing fees,
There'll be nothing left for your family
These Government 'bods' do what they please!

So, enjoy it while it's yours
For it won't be that for long,
Those Governmental jaws
Snap shut! they are exceedingly strong.

Maggie Sparvell

ONE LAST CHANCE

Never give up, never say die,
Keep up and keep on,
All worth a try,
The sun does not give up rising,
The moon never ceases to wane,
Spring follows winter,
As light follows darkness,
All depends on Earth's axis turning,
Ever gave it a thought,
If that came to full stop would gravity cease?
Or the air be full of limbs waving,
Taking off to the great out yonder?
Do not get uptight, no need to panic!
Just do not miss any chances,
It might be your last!
For we are all as the Earth,
In God's plan, not our own,
Well proven history,
He needs no sussing 'mouse',
Just says and it is done!

Anne Mary McMullan

HEADLINE NEWS (5TH OCTOBER 1999)

So long, Mate, see you soon,
Goodbye Dear, don't be late,
Cheerio Love, mind how you go,
'Bye Darling, see you tonight.

So they each said their goodbyes,
On that fateful morning,
Going to work or just a day out,
'Til their lives were changed without warning.

Without fear or premonition,
They boarded the early morning trains,
Red light passed, the point of no return,
Collision, demolition, screeching of the rails.

Twisted metal, twisted bodies,
Sweet oblivion for some,
For others now, a living hell,
Has only just begun.

Another nightmare for those who wait,
A web of trauma spreads itself,
Like a stone rippling on a pool,
To encompass even those who come to help.

Headline news today on all TV
Tomorrow it is history,
Poignant stories in the press,
Replaced by some wars atrocities.

But spare a thought for those,
For whom this day will be,
Forever engraved upon their memory.

Joan Scarisbrick

HEADLINES THE EXPRESS 29TH 1998

$1,000,000 Win a million for the millennium
And £100,000 instantly.
Seeing those headlines I had to buy,
Thinking I must give that a try.
I hurried on home
To check it alone.
I pulled out my card and gave it a scratch
Then I could see I had nothing coming back.
I wondered how many people had won
And were going out that night to have fun
But I bet there were more just like me
Staying in having a cup of tea.

Eileen Kyte

THE BERRY TREE

I wanted you to come and see with me
The wondrous berries that lit up the hedge,
The deep red berries on the hawthorn tree
That marked the boundary of ten acre field.
Our footsteps stretched behind us in the dew
Like dark black shadows on a silver stream.
Tall hedges shone with diamonds; these I knew
Were really angels' teardrops shed at dawn,
Caught in the webs the spiders spin each night.
As we drew near the air was filled with birds,
But on the hawthorn tree no wondrous sight,
The jewel bright berries eaten, every one.

Jeanne Walker

LONELINESS ENDED

What was once a home
Had now become a tomb,
From the cradle onto the grave
The end of his life was doomed.
No one could tell he was gone,
His soul had long departed.
Flesh falling from the bones
Decayed now and rotted.
Only the flies visit in need,
In order that their young may feed.
The room's now filled
With the stench of death,
Drifted upon the noses of others
Taking away their breath,
With this smell in the air
Causing all to create a stir,
Nature had indeed showed its hand,
So that they might bury this
Poor forgotten man.

Pauline Uprichard

BATTERY HENS

I bought some ancient chickens whose useful life had ended.
I only paid £1 each for them - I hope they weren't offended.
To be collected for a 'chop suey' shop those little birds were intended.
I'm glad I 'phoned the farmer up and got them apprehended.

His lad went to the chicken shed with my two large apple cartons;
He put two chickens in each box - I paid and then departed.
When I got my chickens home they really looked absurd.
I understood that from a 'barn' they came - those poor little
                                                                   battery birds.

They'd never been in the daylight - they'd never been on the ground.
Those poor terrified chickens sat there and never made a sound.
Their bottoms looked so pink and sore with not a feather in sight:
No feathers on their necks were seen - they were in a sorry plight.

Their poor beaks had been mutilated to stop them pecking each other.
In a battery cage they had been crammed, one on top of another.
I put them in an enormous shed with three perches at the back.
I had to lift them up to them because they hadn't got the knack.

They must have been kept in a very bright light because in the
                                                    morning I found
The hens had dropped their eggs from their perches to the ground.
Some eggs were distorted, some eggs had no shell;
I'd bought oyster grit to put in their food, which was just as well.

I watched those chickens eating - I'd put their food in a bowl,
But I had to tip the food out into the straw 'cos they couldn't
                                                  pick it up at all.
They were probably used to powdered food with grit and colour added.
I'd let them forage for themselves when their bodies were more padded.

After three weeks I let them out into the garden to roam.
I wanted them to scratch on the lawn and make themselves at home.
They were frightened of the grass at first, but the bird who
was the 'boss'
Neatly grabbed a small white slug which into her mouth she did toss.

They learnt to use the nest boxes when they did show no fear,
And when those hens had laid their eggs a chuckle I did hear.
As those chickens grew their feathers they followed me around -
'Cos I used to dig up lumps of earth and give them worms I'd found.

Diana Kidd

My Last Request

If I could have one more day,
I'd ask my God if I could stay,
to walk again in fields of green,
and live my beautiful country scene;

To walk again in grass so lush
and touch the flowers on the bush,
to saunter through the woodland shade
and see the flowers on parade;

Then onward to the sparkling stream
where life is different, or so it seems,
and watch the timid water vole
peeping from his mud bank hole;

I'd watch the sun filter the trees
sparkling like diamonds on the leaves,
and as my feet walk slowly on
I listen to the skylarks song;

A lazy rabbit hops on by
and nuthatch chicks try to fly,
squirrels dart about in the trees
amongst the busy honey bees;

Silver birches flash the light
making everywhere look bright,
whilst in the fields my feet I find
having left the woods behind;

This is my countryside I'm sure
as I look down at the valley floor,
this is the place that I love best,
it is here that I want to rest;

So my dear wife when I am dead
don't bury me, cremate instead,
and scatter my ashes for ever more
across Alton's Wey Valley floor.

Brian Stewart

EXPOSED VULNERABILITY

She had lost hope;
Her fiancé killed in a violent accident
Exposed a shelless individual
Touched and scarred by all she saw.
Her heart drew back and locked the door,
Her soul did sweat in bitter sorrow,
Her love-want denied
In a frozen no, unrequited to the core.

But pains don't die,
Won't rest in peace.
Symptoms enmass surface to cry,
Seeping through any vacant organ
Looking for openings, and release.

What risk is asked of her as all mankind,
To take a chance as opportunity finds.
Come forth, out of deathly withdrawal.
Come forth, into life renewing.
Come forth, in naked vulnerability;
Believe love supports, each step reviewing.

And like a quivering feather in a gale
She moved.
Faith seized her. Opening in an instance
She saw to choose her long forgotten truth,
To care,
And recognise who shares joins
With the whole eternal dance.

Marion Elvera

IS THIS - THE END?

Okay - so it's over,
I'm going - goodbye!
Alright - you've convinced me,
It's ended - don't try
to stop me, prevent me,
I'm off out the door,
For God's sake stop whinging,
I've heard it before.
I know I'm a failure,
A fraud and a cheat,
That's right, my whole life
has been full of deceit,
You've shouted and screamed it,
Of course I'm to blame,
I'm not denying,
My head hangs in shame.

Oh - please don't start crying,
You know I hate tears,
Here - use my hankie,
Remember the years
when we sang in the sunshine
and danced in the rain,
Come on - look it's raining,
Let's do it again.
No - leave your umbrella,
We'll do a rain dance,
Take my hand - be my partner,
Give me one more chance.

Jim Sargant

ONE LAST CHANCE

I've watched you from across the room
Your eyes have caught me
I cannot escape the thoughts of you
And your name can send shivers.

In my mind I see you look at me
Our eyes meet
You smile, you come over, we talk . . .

But alas, in my mind.

But no! Is fate for once on my side?
I see you look at me
Our eyes meet
Of true happiness,
One
Last
Chance . . .
You blink your eyes, you turn away
I live to grieve another day.

Caz Fisher

GRAVESIDE

This field so tranquil yet bursting with life,
Excited birds, daffodils in bloom, showing that spring is rife.
Stones, like pages of history, date life from the womb of the tomb,
Some of longevity, others ended much too soon.

Yet inscriptions in stone do not reveal a person's true worth,
Nor does it lie buried beneath this earth,
It lives in our hearts by the standards they set,
These our treasured memories, which we should never forget.

For if the promise of eternal life, is broken at the hour of death,
Then every memory is as precious, as each living breath.

T J Dean

ONE LAST CHANCE?

I had a great time last night
The beer was just right.
The company and wine were flowing.
My jokes were hilarious
My antics precarious
My confidence just glowing and growing.

I set the dance floor alight
My feet just took flight
My body was as light as a feather
My thirst grew and grew
But I haven't a clue
Why today I feel under the weather.

I feel proper poorly
My head hurts me sorely
My eyes are bloodshot and flashing
It can't be the drink
As the hospital think
That caused my spectacular crashing
My car is a Rover
I turned it right over
The devil named drink is calling his
           Cash in.

Heather Agius

WHOSE DECISION IS IT, ANYWAY?

She would say they were happy,
day by day,
making no plans.
They agreed to keep it simple,
no commitment, they said.
How things can change!
What rotten timing!

Tomorrow, he goes away,
A new job, a different life.
They'd talked it through,
she understood,
they'd keep in touch.

Now of all times
she needed to think clearly;
but her thoughts were falling
over each other in her head.
Her heart was telling her nothing.

He's nice, loyal, responsible,
he would stick by her
and they would 'work things out'.
But would the pretence of it
soon wear thin?

Tomorrow is her last chance.
He should have the choice
to abandon his plans
or abandon her?
Oh, the pain or pleasure of the risk
to let her secret out!
Should she face it on her own
and deny her child
the chance of a father's love?

Mary Care

THE BEAUTIFUL DAFFODIL

I sign the book as I enter
The club on a Saturday night.
Into the dim music centre,
Without a feature to excite,
No yellows, blues nor magenta,
To lift the gloom and bring delight.
What care I if the room is dull
Or that colours there are none.
I can drink till I am full
And laugh this sad old world to scorn.
Turn my eyes to the wonderful,
Standing there like a golden morn.
Behind the bar, beside the till,
Waits the beautiful daffodil.

Fill my glass with a brimming brew,
Fill it up high without delay.
Her rounded arms with golden hue
Enticingly come into play,
To stir my mind to nimbus stew,
Now my embers of youth are grey.
Yet they might spark again to life,
With that look from summer blue eyes,
In them I see a threat to strife.
Can I reach out and take the prize?
Defy the rules of folk and life?
Shall I be brave, shall I be wise?
Behind the bar, beside the till,
Waits the beautiful daffodil.

Is she too young to be a prey?
Am I too old to be a knight?
When will a spring garden display
Respond to and maybe requite
A barren patch wracked with decay
Long since deprived of youthful might?
Her rounded arms, her rounded thighs,
All made golden by Sol's warm kiss,
Like thunderbolts hurled from the skies,
Mangle my brains and then dismiss,
All hope that in my cleaved heart lies.
Yet, I defy all for that miss,
Behind the bar, beside the till,
Waits the beautiful daffodil.

W Hunt-Vincent

If Only . . .

He said he was sorry that final time,
He took the blame, it was his fault, not mine
But I wouldn't, I couldn't forgive him,
Deep in my heart I did not believe him.

So he rode away on his motorbike,
Roaring off angrily into the night
And I hardened my heart and let him go,
It was just one more row, we didn't know

That fate was waiting on an empty street;
A patch of ice, a tree trunk, running feet,
Too late, not a hope, he had hit his head,
Before help came he was already dead.

Now I am grieving, sobbing and lonely,
Sitting here left with tears and 'if only',
If only I'd hugged him, kissed him that day,
My very last chance; I threw it away.

Valerie Sutton

FAULTS

A father is a father no matter what
You love him even so
Not necessarily agreeing with all that he does
And seeing his faults all too clear

I am his child no matter what
He loves me even so
Not necessarily agreeing with all that I do
And seeing my faults all too clear

But faults are for putting right
That is my belief
Though it is too late for him, he has gone
But me! I'm still here.

L A Smith

ONE LAST CHANCE

One last chance it seems to me
Is offered till eternity,
To make the world a better place
And selfishness indeed efface.
Good intentions we know well
Simply pave the road to hell.

Let's rather think in terms of heaven
And take the opportunities given
To rid the world of evil
And overcome the devil,
Turn what appears reversible
From hopeless to impossible.

It is the only way to live
Seeking always to forgive,
Doing everything one can
To improve the life of man.
Even those of little brain
Should know this chance won't come again!

Joyce Parker

A GAME OF CHANCE

He begged me for another go,
Undying love he swore.
He wheedled and he pleaded,
A haunted look he wore.

But my arms stayed firmly folded,
Emphatically I shook my head,
This game was really over
No matter what he said.

I'd heard the familiar stories
A hundred times before,
Now I needed to be strong enough
To watch him reach the door.

As he trailed sadly from the room,
I heard him softly say,
'With two hotels on Mayfair, Mum,
I could have *really* made you pay!'

Jeannie Price

REPENTANCE

Humanity had dreamt of glory
The conquest of Heaven and Earth
The ascent towards spiritual magnificence
And a vision of eternal belief
But dreams can be fatal weapons
A curse to all that they touch
The Earth is an ecological testament
Where humanities guilt can be found

Rainforests are systematically gutted
Thus the lungs of the Earth disappear
Crops succumb to the chemical pestilence
And wither with the flowers and trees
Oceans are muted with sadness
Rivers are swallowed by death
The sun shines upon this criminal chaos
With a haunting parental disgust

The atmosphere bleeds with pollution
The sky is serrated and torn
The climate has declared a mutiny
A war of aggression and spite
As the ice-caps retreat to obscurity
The sea will steal from the land
And hurricanes will savage the continents
Tearing prayers from the innocent homes

While strangling the voice of the faithful
Droughts blossom with famine and disease
A new world is waiting anonymously
Where only deserts can flourish and thrive
Though armed with the tools of destiny
But like a virus the humans destroyed
Wildlife may be served with extinction
As the patience of nature rebels

The millennium offered repentance
One last chance to pardon the past
This truce is the final instalment
That mankind and nature will have
With belief has the arbitral agent
The future can be laden with gold
So humanity can still dream of glory
And the comfort of perennial peace

David Bridgewater

REALITY BITES

No need to say
what's written on my face
we've nowhere to turn
in a room full of corners
and since when has our future been as rosy
as the cheeks of a teething baby
shall we roll up our sleeves and get on with it
for our debtors will not forgive us
or wipe the slate clean with a white flag
did we don a familiar coat
against the winds of change
without ever reading the price tag
this morning I awoke
as blue as the Prussian sky
with silver moon suspended
and realised that I
was still pretending to be
that poor defenceless optimist
savaged by reality.

Heather Kirkpatrick

ONE LAST CHANCE

One last chance to get it sorted; the future beckons like a burning light.
We must be bold in all we do, let's hope we get it right.
We have reached the edge; we have come so far.
As we step onward we are fearful; will we reach our star?
The future is like a black hole; we are filled with trepidation.
Who cares what people think, it is only our reputation.
I only know our lives must change, to meet with the times.
Maybe we have got it right, maybe there will be a sign?
Who would have thought how simple, it made me feel like a thief.
Once we had it all sorted out, we heaved a big sigh of relief.
I suggest you read between the lines all you can.
As usual I am hiding things, it's all part of the plan.
Centuries will pass and life will go on.
One day someone will read this, and wonder what was wrong?
As we reach the new millennium, I wish you all the best.
There is a story in here somewhere; will you pass the test?
Look very carefully; remember we are all in the same boat.
One last chance to sort it out, before this all goes up in smoke.

Ken Mills

DRINK UP MY FRIEND
(The definition of a drinker.
A filter between a brewer and a sewer.)

Drink up my friend the end is nigh
Have another little drink, before ye die.
There ain't no bars in heaven yer know
So have another drink before yer go.

There once was a chap called Jesus, who in the bible so they do say.
Once performed a great miracle and turned water into red wine one day.
Well you too may equal his efforts, though you may think it no
                                                        marvellous feat.
For you too can turn good ale into water, when you go into t' toilet
                                                        toneet

So bless this my drink Oh Lord Divine
You who changes water into wine
And bless also Lord all those worthy men
Who now will change it back again!

Charlie Walker

A Portrait Of A Policeman

We are pleased to perceive our policeman
Patiently pounding the paves;
Proudly protecting the populous.
A patriotism he portrays.

He does not preach or patronise,
A policy he painstakingly pursues.
Perhaps he's not all perfect
But a profitable product procures.

He's a peacemaker and persuader,
A practising political paragon.
He's primarily a crime preventer
But a polite paternal person.

Where pilfering or pornography are practised
And a permissive phobia pervades:
When parishioners are privately petrified,
His professionalism he pleasantly purveys.

William Milne

REBORN

A walk to the postbox
    with fond letter in hand
A trip to the rubbish tip
    with old garbage and sand
A day clipping hedges
    or mowing the lawn
A bonfire with leaves and old
    wood newly sawn
A morning having coffee with a
    very old friend
Or wrapping a parcel my
    grandchild to send
Time just spent watching as
    the birds feed
Depriving the lawn of the
    newly sown seed
Minutes spent watching raindrops
    fall from the skies
Or the smell from the kitchen
    of fresh apple pies
Furniture gleaming from polish
    just sprayed
The sight of the family around the
    table newly laid
Things I considered intrusions
    I now welcome with glee
Telephones, faxes and offers
    for free
These things now so precious
    because I've been given a second chance
From six feet under fertilising
    the plants

I awaken each day with a smile on
    my face
And thank God in his wisdom He's
    deferred my place.

Gloria Hargreaves

THE VOICE OF ALL VOICES

A one eyed bearded mercenary, with a sharp blade in his hand
Said 'Cross my palm with silver, or I'll kill you where you stand
Dead men tell no stories, dead men tell no lies
But the horror of their ending, is often captured in their eyes'

The murder and mayhem rages on, and the weak and mighty fall
As little children play in pools of blood, oblivious to it all
And 'the voice of all voices' speaks, and chills me to the bone
Proclaiming 'Your time is coming to an end, your time will not be long'

I met a gypsy woman, with hair and eyes as black as coal
She had the fires of hell, burning in her heart, and the devil in her soul
We made love under a full moon, lost ourselves in love's delights
But her joy soon turned to sorrow, on that hot midsummer's night

For while resting she had a vision, in her 'mind's eye' something
she saw
She warned 'Your time is coming to an end, of this you can be sure'
And 'the voice of all voices' speaks, and chills me to the bone
Proclaiming 'Your time is coming to an end, your time will not be long'

The seven wonders of my homeland, cry out with voices so forlorn
'Come home! Come home! Ye wayward son, to the shores where
you were conceived and born'
Under dark skies I stand alone and stare, at grey waves that roll
in from the sea
And as they lap upon the shore, I hear them whisper gently

'Come and join us! Come and join us! It does not matter anymore
For your time is coming to an end, of this you can be sure'
And 'the voice of all voices' speaks, and chills me to the bone
Proclaiming 'Your time is coming to an end, your time will not be long'

E D Jones

Spiritual Love

When death holds your hand and your time is through
you may have loved money and possessions, but did they love you?
Were they just false friends, who made your love blind
because they never shed a tear, when you left them behind
or were you the one, who believed in real love and good deeds?
You left a lot of sorrow, but the memory of you still feeds
the security of your love, still lives today
for the ones your life touched, followed your way.

T Allbright

HANDS OF REPROACH

Born before the opportunity
to fail an eleven plus exam.
Condemned by a lineage of hired farm hands
to receiving the skeleton of an education
for a career of manual, unskilled jobs.
He considered me to be so clever
for I was nourished by library fiction
and often acted as unofficial second
to struggling contestants on TV quiz shows.
He tossed tactical words of encouragement
rather than hinder me during homework
towards the prize of three bashful 'O' levels
and a job with prospects.

Raised in the honourable north Cumberland villages
where fathers with forearms sculpted by labour
and mothers heavy with childbearing and housework
raised families on tradition, common sense and stern love.
He was too innocent for the town
and the mutiny of flower power
when I became old enough to ignore his advice.
His temper rose like mercury
each time I enjoyed records too potent for his ears.
We argued as passionately as politicians
with both of us too stubborn to compromise
and selfish to expect my mother to arbitrate.
Yet he winced at the sight of each bruise
I earned from games of rugby and football.

A clown for company, comrade for confidences
to whom harvesting friendships came as natural as breathing.
A miracle that such a lean body
could sustain all the love he had to share.
It came as a shock though no great surprise
when at the age of fifty-seven
his heart collapsed under the burden.

I still wear his wristwatch;
the second hand his finger wagging,
the hour and minute hands reprimands
for how much I am still managing to get it all wrong.

Stephen Atkinson

BIRTHDAY GIRL

Waiting by the cinema, tossing a rugby ball
In the early summer evening air.
Then she came, my special lady,
Walking on air on her birthday.

She could not have been more lovely,
Walking by the beach on her own May day,
The wind almost blowing her brown hair into my eyes,
Soft-voiced as she asked if I felt cold.

Inside, sampling drink no 70,
We have the same seafood inclination:
Her pink prawns lounging on ciabatta,
My haddock a chip off the old block.

Bowled over by my success in tenpin territory,
Life in the slow lane beckons.
She also cast her lot, encouraging me
As my Jericho of skittles fell.

I smiled at her happiness,
Eager and bright-eyed as a child,
On this day of remembering
Her, and how special she is.

David Tallach

DREAMER

They call you a dreamer my child my girl
They say you just sit with your head in a whirl
They say you should be working not filling your head
With thoughts of the stories you heard or read
Your report said 'Good work when she is not in a dream
Works well alone, works well in a team.'

So what shall we do my little girl
How shall we stop those dreams unfurl
I won't say stop, just put them aside
Until you have time to sit and abide
Work when you must and dream when you can
Then come and tell Daddy all about them.

Peter S Sims

LIFE LOVE
(For Mark)

Thirty years
More than half our lives
Travelling together
The winding road
A joyous journey

Along the way
The pain of paths diverging
Seeking different destinations
The journey interrupted

After sadness and despair
The joy of finding anew
The special sensations
Life love returns

What were all the tears about
A sense of wasted steps
A need for different exploration

God knows I tried to understand
The pain the grief
The sense of hopelessness

Time heals all wounds
I am grateful for new growth
Yet memory lingers
Catches me unawares
A twinge of pain
Flitting through my mind
On butterfly wings

Or
A deep ache
Falling like a stone
Through the well of thought
The disturbance lingering
The entire body of water displaced

Dark memory settles swiftly now
Tranquil
It lies undisturbed
Contained within its own space
Restored
I surface into sunlight
Rejoin the winding road

Sue Parritt

DESERT ROSE

True love is like a desert rose
Whose beauty viewed in an arid place
Imbues the heart with joy in those
Whose way is hard or lacking grace

Or like a spring on a hot summer's day,
Or a shady bower in a quiet retreat
Refreshing the traveller along the way:
Both without price, in measure replete

My heart was touched by love like this
In youth, when life was dark and riven;
And still in age remains the bliss
Of their sweet love so freely given

Alan Compton

You Were Abused

I looked into your eyes and I could see
you were abused during infancy
The pain you were made to bear
could be forever in your stare
child abuse is a wicked game
but you were not to blame
Not knowing who did this to you
or the reason he was so bad
now we have met I am so very very glad
As not all men should be held with such disdain
for with me you will trust and love again
Trust and love will grow from your sorrow
and live on in you for tomorrow and tomorrow

Alan M Brewster

A MOTHER

A mother is there to understand
She is there to give you a hand
A mother is there, when you are sad
She even cares when you are bad
She loves us all the young and old
A mother is there when we feel cold
Thank you Lord for my mother
I wouldn't swap her for any other
A mother helps you anytime, anywhere
I just call her she's always there
And when you fall into deep trouble
She's there for you at the double
She picks you up when you feel down
She even does it without a crown
And when you find that you have no friend
She sticks with you till the end.

C Johnston

FROM THE KITCHEN WINDOW

Her eyes saw fingers fumble,
drop the screw,
hasten to retrieve before the son noticed.
      Her mind remembered
          countless nimble-fingered jobs:
          safe hands that held a rugby ball
          nursed a child
          loved gently.
Her heart perceived a priceless gift
in the stooped figure,
anxious to conceal all frailties.

Her eyes smiled warmth as they met his -
seeing no flaws,
seeing only his sure and generous
handling of life:
seeing strength and promise
in the helping hands:
seeing her lover,
loving what she saw.

Pat McDonald

Distingúe

Puccini, Rossini, Debussy,
What is in a name?
Ravel, Brahms and Janàcek,
All have claim to fame.
From Opera to Concerto,
Tone Poem to Symphony,
Haydn, Mozart and Beethoven,
These must surely be -
The Fathers of great Music,
They dominate the stage.
With Beethoven's 'Fidelio',
When Opera was the rage.

Mozart's 'Idomeneo'
Was evidence of his Skill,
With 'Don Giovanni' and 'Figaro',
'Die Zauberflöte until,
Schumann, Schubert, Chopin,
Mendelssohn and Berlioz,
By their uncanny mastery,
The Romantic era rose.
Wagner's 'Flying Dutchman',
'Rienzi' and 'The Ring',
'Die Meistersinger's passion,
When drama was the thing.

'Russian and Ludmilla',
Bearing Glinka's name,
Rimsky-Korsakov Tchaikovsky,
Bringing Russia fame.
Sibelius, Grieg and Mahler,
Great composers in their right,
Gustav Holst and Delius,
Vaughan-Williams with Elgar's might.
Strauss, Stravinsky and Dvorák
All have left a legacy,
But for them we'd be the poorer,
On that note we can agree.

Doris E Farran

GRANDMA

From out of the shadows I suddenly saw
Somebody whom I felt I had seen long before
She touched my arm gently, and just stood quietly near
As if she was saying, 'I do understand how you're feeling my dear.'

For a moment I held out my hand for her touch
I needed to feel that reassurance so much.
That elderly stranger, who I did not know
Reminded me of my dear Grandma of long, long ago.

She was kind, she was gentle, she was loving, but stern
And she taught her young grandchild all she needed to learn.
She taught me to read, and taught me to write
And stood by my bed and kissed me goodnight.

She taught me to knit and she taught me to sew
Because being left-handed was hard, long ago.
She had so much patience with that little one
And I loved her so for all she had done.

Many years have now passed since Grandma was here
Yet while I have memories, there's nothing to fear.
She was loving and tender, and she set me free
And she will always be near and mean all things to me.

Sue Goodman

93 YEARS YOUNG!

I have a dear Aunt Minnie
Who's so very dear to me
Such a kind and gracious lady
As alert as one can be
She listens with avid interest

And want's to know the score
She always has a kind word
No matter what you do
She remembers all the good times
And the dates and names gone by
She finds the modern ways of life
Always bring a cautious smile!
She treasures memories in her heart
And we love her all the more.

Margaret Luckett-Curtis

VALENTINE STREET

There's a wild eyed moon in Sailortown,
And a scented shadow in a sable gown,
Fastened against the wind from winter's throne,
That chills the pale throat that his kiss had known.

There's a vacant heart in Sailortown,
And a feline figure swiftly gliding down
Amid sounds from the blind ebony sea,
And the water dancing low by the quay.

There's a broken dream in Sailortown,
Below Ben Madigan's star-crested crown,
That goes softly to the west and exile
With the stolen memory of a smile.

Martin Magee

JUST WORDS OF LOVE

Clichés, just trite expressions I heard a cynic say
like, my love for you is going to last forever and a day,
or I cannot live without you and my love will never die
is expressed with deep emotion and a never-ending sigh.

At times there is a longing whenever I'm alone,
to hear those trite expressions in your gentle loving tone,
for they filled me with a feeling of such wonderful delight
when you whispered all those words of love your arms holding me
tight.

So my darling, though you're far-away your letters I will keep,
and read the words you've written wishing I could hear you speak
your feelings, written on each page so heartfelt yet full of,
every cliché ever uttered signed, with my undying love.

Mary Hoy

REMEMBERING FIRST LOVE

It seems there's many loves in life which touch our inward souls
Enriching passing of the years with strands of shining gold.
The love of child to parent, of husband unto wife.
The burdens eased by sharing when the path is strewn with strife.
Each love fulfils its purpose as we walk along life's way,
However brief the contact - the love will ever stay.
First love with so much magic fills lives with joy untold,
And should that first love falter along youth's tortuous road -
The anguish felt is bitter and sorrow seems complete,
But through it comes a strengthening, which will not own defeat.
Life's tapestry continues and further joys are sown,
Another love - a lasting love within each heart is grown.
My dear it happened in our lives a brief and lovely time,
Remembered with nostalgia now, when age has passed its prime.
When after fifty years had passed we met again and there -
We found a friendship lasting, which both our partners share.
Affection stands the test of time and friendship's ties unite
With cords of past and present which nothing now can blight.
In memories and sharing of the many missing years,
The loved ones that we married who now we hold so dear.
I'm grateful that we met again tho' fifty years have gone
And youth has passed the non return - but memories linger on.
We catch a glimpse of time now past - remembering as friends
And know with joy and thankfulness that memories do not end.

Patricia Ruffle

GATHERING DUST

This work of mine could gather dust,
But writing poetry is a must,
Silly in rhyme, but serious in thought,
Based on my life and experiences -
That's something, that cannot be bought.
Now I'm retired life is taken at a slower pace,
But take in the news and observe the human race.
My poetry and rhyme I like to share,
It raises a smile - keeps me aware.
Relations, neighbours, friends far and near,
Have to listen to my nostalgia and verse,
At least once a year.
The response that I get is varied,
But there's never any gloom,
No one yet has told me to go lay
Down in a dark room!
So to conclude and I hopefully trust,
'My poetry and rhyme will never gather dust.'

Dennis Roy Judd

Friendship

A friend is always there,
They may need you to care.

Remember when you give love,
You will receive love.

It may not be in an instant,
But within time the realisation is proven.
That love will be returned,
Not once but tenfold.

Irene Morgans

DERWENT

There was a young duck called Dillon
whose coat was bright green and vermillion.
His favourite tea was lapschong shu
which he sipped through a straw,
stripped with blue.

He couldn't fly and couldn't swim
so he sat on the floor with a curious grin.
Seasons changed and still he stared
at the others who flew by without a care.

Amy Phillips

THE BATTLE OF THE BULGE
(A dialogue between a Fatty and a Thinny)

F All the smartest dresses are
   For women who are svelte and trim,
   And I want to follow fashion.
   Will you tell me how to slim?

T Exercise of course will do it,
   But you'll find it very hard.
   It will take a lot of jogging
   To get rid of all that lard.

   Or there's diet; no more butter,
   Cream, or anything that's sweet.
   Do you think you have the will power
   When there's something nice to eat?

F But I've heard there is another,
   Easy way to make one thin.
   Surgeons can remove the blubber,
   Sucking underneath the skin.

   This appears to me the surest
   Way to tackle weight reduction.
   No more exercise and diet!
   I will go for liposuction.

T Do be careful, liposuction
   Has been known to leave some lumps.
   Would you like to see your tummy
   Landscaped into vales and humps?

   Anyway, I think you worry
   Far too much about your figure.
   You are really quite attractive;
   Just take care you get no bigger.

F   What you say's an indication
Fat and thin are poles apart.
I am only 'quite attractive',
You are elegant and smart . . .

I am going to start a movement,
Making fat the thing to be.
When it's trendy you'll be sorry
You are not as big as me!

Reine Errington

FOR THE LOVE OF . . .
FAMILY

Tah Too . . . the alarm clock rings at four-forty-five.
I hear it . . . though I do not hear . . .
Turning, weary, into my pillow . . . I try . . .
To ignore, but instinct steers,
reluctant hand;

Gropingly, switched off . . . the silence screams . . .
Touch-feel hand . . . stretched out . . . till found.
Glasses, teeth, hearing aid, all creamed
Into place, no sound
disturbs . . .

Slippers slipped, while the white moon plays,
Patterns on my counterpane, sneaking chill
Silvered shivers, which are made
Sharp. Bed-warm lingering still
in my bones.

Stumbling stealth . . . I screech the oaken stool . . .
Breaking the silence of silent night . . .
Slicing with sound the calm, the cool . . .
Greying, early morning light
approaching day.

Fumbling freezer lid, for frozen breakfast buns . . .
Rushing water, cheese wrap tear . . .
Automotive movement . . . mechanic run . . .
Sleepwalk-work . . . as I prepare
. . . morning ritual

Then the thump of rushing movement, booms . . .
Doors dashed open, floorboards creak . . .
Radios sound, in once quiet rooms . . .
I hear their voices, as they speak
in passing.

Kettle hisses . . . coffee smells, and toaster toasts and pops . . .
Butter smears . . . microwave peeps . . .
Egg machine steams, then stops . . .
And, one by one, they stagger, creep
Into the kitchen.

The workday routine, of a caring home . . .
Hand-turn helping and support . . .
No-one abandoned, left alone . . .
Everything, just as it ought . . .
to be.

Brenda Robson-Eifler

THE NEW ARRIVAL

Congratulations, both of you
On the birth of your little one
She may not be the only baby
Underneath the sun
But she is just adorable
A miracle come true
And in this world she is unique
A part of both of you

That's what makes her special
No other quite the same
There was no one like her before
Nor ever will again
So nurture her with lots of love
On her your wisdom pour
And she will always be so proud
That she is *yours*

Maureen Quirey

DIVINE LOVE

Have you told Him you love Him,
Have you told Him you care,
Have you told Him you need Him,
and you're glad that He's there.
There to uphold you,
and carry you through.
Have you told Him you love Him,
because He first loved you.

Ken Price

JEWEL IN MY CROWN

The head on my shoulder, gently sighs
And snuggles so slightly deeper.
I gaze with content at the beauteous sleeper
And hold her like a most precious prize.

The scent of her hair softly lingers
Bewitched, she has me spellbound.
I'm careful not to wake her with a sound
As I caress her tiny curling fingers.

She is the jewel in my crown
Outshining any diamond or pearl,
She means more than anything in the world.
When I look into her eyes of hazel-brown
I never want to lay her down,
She is my darling baby girl.

Keith Tissington

SEASON'S GREETINGS

I went to the shops before Christmas
Nothing special on my mind
Anything on my Christmas list
Or unusual things to find

While shopping in the market
I saw a Santa on a string
Thought it might amuse my cats
They like that sort of thing

I found a few things to cross off my list
My shopping bags began to fill
Tired but happy it was time for home
Most of my cash in their till

The first thing I'd do when I arrived home
Was make a pot of tea
I dumped my bags on the kitchen floor
But a surprise was waiting for me

Yo-ho-ho, and a merry Christmas
Came from the pile of bags on the floor
My Santa on a string had a voice of his own
I nearly shot out of the door

I now realise he just needs a bump
Then my Santa his deep voice will find
But when I dumped him on my kitchen floor
Christmas greetings were far from my mind

So if you're tired or lonely
Don't feel sad or full of woe
For Santa won't forget you
Merry Christmas, Yo-ho-ho.

Peggy Hunter

MY ANGEL LOVE

Every morning before sunrise
I wait for you to open your hazel eyes
Followed by your warm smile that begins every day
And makes me feel happy in your magical way

Then you give me a passionate kiss
Before you set off to work at the children's hospice
In a child's final days you give them your very best
As they wait for God to take them to rest

It takes someone special for work of this kind
And you've the gift that's so hard to find
At least parents know why you are there
Their children are receiving the very best care.

Keith Large

NIGHT-TIME BEVERAGE

I'm tiring now,
In need of beverage
As I slip up the stairs
And into your room.
You know I'll come
When I need a cup
Of your dark brown
West Indian flavour.
I enfold you,
A petite, wide naked cup,
As I sip your warm fragrance
And drink down your
Rich, dark tones,
Punctuated by
Corridor noises,
Making this illicit
Night-time beverage - delicious!

Joe Hughes

COMPUTER CAT

I *know* you want attention, little friend,
But these are letters I have *got* to send.
You see one printing now. Yes, if it's fun,
Stick in your paw - no little mouse will run.

Say, on this desk there's not much room, you'll find:
For cat games it is simply not designed.
Oh well, just don't walk on the keyboard, please . . .
Oops! How you open data files with ease!

Let's close that. And this document of mine
Does not require the figure 'eighty-nine'.
I'd better save before you change still more . . .
That's *my* mouse you are patting with your paw,

Not your kind - sadly it won't run away,
Though that's the favourite game you like to play.
All right, you might as well climb on my lap . . .
Or on my shoulder, snuggling little chap.

Yes, I can type with one hand, I suppose,
While I support you on the perch you chose
And listen to you roaring in my ear -
Don't you have things to say? You're such a dear!

Perhaps stop digging in your claws, my pet?
You haven't fallen off my shoulder yet!
Er, Puss, you are a heavy cat, you know,
And this one-handed typing goes so slow!

'But what is more important?' you might say.
I surely don't want you to go away!
I wish you to feel wanted, that is true,
And what an honour to be holding you!

So should I shut it down just for your sake?
Was that the point that you have tried to make?
We'll sit together, you upon my knee -
We won't be here forever, you and me.

Anne Sanderson

THE BUS!

A splendid creature is The Bus, if you and one should meet,
But sadly they're a rarity and seldom cruise the street;
Your patience is a virtue and won't hurt you if you drop
From hunger, and from waiting for a fortnight at the stop:

But never mind, you're still resigned to catch one if it comes,
And tell of the excitement to your mother and your chums,
You've set up camp despite the damp, and dogs which can disturb,
Destined to wait for Bus or fate, just camping on the curb!

All night the traffic rumbles on, disturbing dreams and sleep;
And every time it rains the drains cause floods a metre deep;
You keep a lookout just in case The Bus should pass you by,
With patience still unblemished, and your spirit's soaring high!

You think you see one coming, an oasis in the sand,
Do everything that's possible to stop it with your hand:
But due to malnutrition, lack of sleep and drink, you find
The Bus was just a mirage, and a rotten trick of mind.

The public are quite wonderful, and keep your spirits strong
Maintaining reassurance that The Bus'll come along;
Just when you've given up all hope, and patience is long spent,
You've packed up your belongings, and taken down the tent -

- A creature whizzes past you, which makes you really cuss,
Because it was the rarest of a species called, The Bus!

Nicholas Winn

OUR PATCH

Our dog Patch did the strangest things
Once he thought he was sprouting wings.
One summer's day when we went away
Auntie Pat and Uncle Paul had Patch for the day.

It was the middle of the afternoon
When Auntie Pat could be seen to swoon.
She saw a blur flash past her way.
'Whatever was that?' she was heard to say.
'I can't be sure what you just saw
But I think it was Patch who flew past our door.'

They both raced outside to see the dog.
And they shook their heads all agog.
'Well fancy that,' said Auntie Pat
'That dog's a fool,' said Uncle Paul.

He had jumped out of a window high
The silly dog thought he could fly.
Our Patch stood up and let out a bark.
He had leapt to the ground for a doggy lark.
Auntie Pat said, 'Patch come in and have your tea,
You funny old dog, you'll be the death of me!'

Linda Hurdwell

A STRING IN THE TAIL

Walking 'midst the cows, I sense something's wrong,
One's leaving the herd, apparently no wish to belong,
It's time for this wild-eyed heifer, to be a first calver,
Instinct tells me though, we have a calving drama.

Calling to her unborn calf, she looks for a quiet place,
For privacy to give birth naturally, in her own space,
On her side with neck stretched up, she bears down,
Back legs first, a breech, get on or young may drown.

Quietly I ease calf free, clear membrance off its head,
Cow's up instantly, on me she really wants to tread,
Head down she charged, butting me square in the chest,
And threw me into a big nettle bed, to give me a rest.

Peter Sell

TURN-A-ROUND

Come my daughter
For a treat
Clean hands and face
Stout shoes on feet.
The circus has come
We've clowns to see
Impatiently she waits for me.
Hold my hand the road to cross
You're in my care
And I'm the boss.

Come my mother
For a treat
I have tickets
For two theatre seats.
Spectacles, sweets
And locked door key
Impatiently she waits for me.
A busy road on arm I cross
I'm in her care
Now she's the boss.

Ann Martin

THE JOURNEY

Blacker than black sneaks the midnight prowler,
Slinking past neat, low walls,
Only pausing briefly to sniff at dustbins
Where possible remains of last night's fish and chip supper
Tease the taste buds.
For an unexpected snack is always welcome
Before the serious business of the night begins.

Now, when mere mortals sleep,
The world belongs to you
As with whiskers trembling with anticipation, head down,
You plod purposefully along hard, dark pavements.
Where are you going?
Evidence of certainty is clear in every step you take.
You know well the path you travel
And the reward that awaits you on completion of your
solitary journey.
Are you keeping a date with a mate?
A secret assignation?
A feline council meeting?
Perhaps an emergency assembly to discuss the problems
of the increased fox population?

O beloved, mysterious friend! I'm solely yours.
And yet you're never truly mine,
Although you deign to eat and sleep under my roof
And grudgingly suffer an occasional cuddle.
Yet you still remain
Distant, aloof and enigmatic -
A curiosity of time.

Eileen M Pratt

GRANDCHILDREN

Grandchildren are a wonder to behold;
A colourful rainbow with a crock of gold.
To watch over you fills me with great joy,
Whether it's three little girls or one little boy.

I love to see you arrive for the day.
I love to hear the funny things that you say.
Your active minds keep me on my toes;
How the day will go, nobody knows.

Rice crispies in the kitchen, flour on the floor;
Chocolate on your faces and some on the door.
We'll always find something to keep us busy
Even if it's dancing 'til we're quite dizzy.

Dens in the garden, mud pies fit to eat.
'Mind those stones, you've nothing on your feet.'
A wicked glint and turned up nose,
How do I avoid that well-aimed hose?

The magic of your hand held in mine,
Your silky soft skin and eyes that shine,
Some of the memories I'll hold and treasure
Knowing you all is such a pleasure.

It won't be long before you're all fully grown
Off to seek futures of your own.
I'll think of you often wherever you may be
As valuable branches of our family tree.

Be happy with your lives and in all that you choose
Because you're the ones with nothing to lose.
Fill it with love and always show that you care
For then you will find a life beyond compare!

Ruth Robinson

WITHIN . . .

Within the bosom of your beating breast,
Within the warmth of your embrace I now rest,
Within the mist of fragrant perfume we permeate,
Within our bodies, entwined, we are one; soulmate.
Within your loving arms I now lay,
Within our essence, as one we shall stay,
Within ardent passion, as one; entwined,
Within our bodies, hearts, soul and mind.
Within our naked flesh we now lay adorn,
Within our bodily form to which we were born.
Within loving embrace; mind and soul in playful thought,
Within a berth of soft petals with tenderness covert;
Within the lustful spell with which we feast,
Within the lover; beauty and beast.
Within love's passion, beneath a scarlet sky.
Within my lover, with whom I lie.
Within the sacred temple of such purity found,
Within the sanctuary of Mother Earth's holy ground.
Within the scent of earth's fragrant perfume,
Within our love; Mother Earth, our lover's tomb.

Marc Tyler

To My Darling Wife, Maureen

When I am gone from this place,
far away, into the shadowed land,
no more to look upon thy face,
or hold thee gently by the hand,
and see the truth there in thine eye,
of your love, steadfast and true,
that I defiled with constant lies,
was faithless, weak and selfish too.
I hurt you badly, gave you pain,
heartbreak sadness and despair.
O! that I could live my life again,
and all my past misdeeds repair.
But time will not return the years,
not for my longing, not for my tears.

Still in the playground as a child was I;
but time has taught me how to grow,
to understand the wherefore and the why,
and I'm more sorry than you'll ever know . . .
Now I grow old . . . grow old and grey,
let not my voice fade in your ears,
my love go from your heart.
Weep not for me, and shed no tears
when I am gone, and we're apart,
but think about the things I've said.
Remember me when I am dead,
do not let me die.

Huw Parry

AFTER THE MILLENNIUM

The grass will still be green,
The sky will still be blue,
The wind will always blow -
And cows will always chew.

Birds will always sing -
And rain will always fall,
Whatever we say or do,
Creepies will always crawl.

The sun, the moon and stars
Will always be the same
Flowers will always bloom,
It's people who must change.

The future can be altered,
By folk like you and me,
The world could become one country -
Just you wait and see.

To help us find the answers,
We need to understand,
Other nations' problems,
And give a helping hand.

And take a tip from one above
To always add a little love.

Milly Hatcher

AUTUMN

Have you ever gone walking on a cold Autumn night
When it's not quite dark and it isn't quite light
Heard the cold autumn breeze
soughing through the red leaf coloured trees
And there along the street in the darkening day
you see a warm yellow light to brighten the way
As you approach, you see a welcoming sight
where the curtains aren't drawn against
the cold of night
For there in that room as you pause to look
People are watching TV or reading a book
Do you wish you were with them in the warm yellow glow
instead of standing outside as the cold winds blow
and as you stand there in the deepening gloom
longing to be in that bright warm room
the curtains get drawn against the cold of night.
Blocking you off from that heart-warming sight
So you set off again, going on your way
into the night and the fading day

Reginald T Dennis

My Last Goodbye

The moon has fallen from the sky
Its broken shards around me lie
Stygian blackness is my now
Wrinkled lines bestrew my brow.

The sun has turned its back on day
In mourning for the moon's lost ray
The stars that twinkled in the night
Have lost their sweet poetic light

The clocks have lost their timely ticks
No wax is fuelling candles' wicks
With total blackness now my thrall
What use have I for life at all?

Birdsong, which heralded the dawning
Has sadly died with lack of morning
The birds have spread their wings and flown
Insects and bees no longer drone

Silence has descended on a senseless world
The flowers and the leaves are staying furled
Nothing to tell them of a new-born day
They are left to die where e'er they lay

Turn my eyes in and let me be!
Leave me to die in jeopardy
For no life is left now you have gone
And no light exists where your light shone!

Royston E Herbert

COLOUR YOUR LIGHT

I want to paint you with my words
But you are a language beyond my art.
I wish with each stroke of my pen
I could colour your light
And create an image that is but an essence.
A portrait that only I can see
And others can only interpret.
But I have not the skill
To paint even what you've done.

Jason Senior

GETTING NOWHERE

Walking alone while hopes and dreams,
Drip away and wash down the roads in small rivers.
Sitting at the edge of the ocean,
Feet dangling in the sea of broken promises.
Past faces appear and disappear in the mist.
I want to hold on to them but I am bound,
Not by anything material but by the present.
How can we repeat the past?
I would even go through the pain of recent years,
Just to get back.
Back to what I know.
My old school friends,
All heading upstream to the land of success.
And as I turn to view what lies in store for me,
A deep dark void glares back.
Panic and fright well up inside,
But I'm slipping into the ocean,
And being dragged by the spiteful current.
Into the dark.
Slowly nausea sweeps over me,
It's so dark.
Then I wake to find myself back,
Back at the beginning.
Walking alone while hopes and dreams,
Drip away and wash down the roads in small rivers.
Do you ever get the feeling that you're on a treadmill
Getting nowhere fast.

Claire Sanderson

WEATHER FORECAST

We laughed as we walked and we giggled and talked
About all sorts of subjects and then;
Well, you know how girls chat all about this and that
And of course we talked lots about men!
She asked, 'What's the chance of a lasting romance
With your date that I've heard all about?'
I thought for a while then I said, with a smile,
'I don't know; but it's fun finding out!

I'll meet him tonight and if things turn out right
We'll be hitting the high spots together.
I'll just have to see what the future will be,
But that all depends on the weather.'
'D'you mean it all goes if it rains or it snows
Or if it's too cold or too hot?'
But I had to explain that I don't mind the rain;
It's whether he's wealthy or not!

Dennis Turner

MILLENNIUM EVE

Those of us who are older dreamed in our teens
That the year 2000 was outside our pale
And now it has reached us - crept up as it were
You can see from tonight it has caused quite a stir
There's a time for reflection in all men's lives
From William the Conqueror to Henry the VIII and his wives
Through to Gladstone, Disraeli and the Great Wars too
What's in a calendar - it gives us a clue of the agelessness of time
We're just passing through - mere dots on the landscape
But we must make our mark
We are great inventors - we just need a spark
To fire our human mind
But progress has galloped like a runaway horse
The rag and bone merchant is staggered of course
For fifty years on there are men on the moon
Football is glorified, divorce is rife
Cocooned in our cars there is more stress and strife.

Computers are championed they will rule us all
IT is not scone, jam and a cuppa at the Sunday School stall
My message to you is keep your feet on the ground
With all the distraction dangers abound
Would it not be fascinating to just take a peep
At the year 3000 if only in sleep
To meet with a Martian and show him Stonehenge
And discuss shillings and pence florins and pounds
Oh a curse on the kilo, the metre, the hectare
Bring back the mile and the gill - they taste like nectar
Bring back the values we once understood
Modern day man is lost in a wood
Where the way out is pitted with potholes and flack
It is so easy to be led from the track.

And so be resolute on this memorable night
And live life to the full and not to lose sight
Of our glorious ancestry and there's still more to come
You see - the world is not enough
On the morrow arise refreshed from your snug
I hope you avoided the Millennium Bug!

M C Davies

'FLIGHTS OF FANCY'

I close my eyes, in darkness I fly
Severing the earthly bonds I soar
Above treetops, over mountains high
Across distant lands and oceans roar.

I see places, I have seen before
Faraway places, I see anew
I see old friends, I have known before
I see strangers there, who welcome you.

I speed through space, I travel in time
The past and present in total flight
I fly in fantasy in every clime
I cross the boundaries of the night.

Even before Morpheus takes me
I find I can travel anywhere
I solve any problems that I see
I take those journeys without a care.

Terry Daley

IF I SHOULD LOSE YOU

If I should lose you, the rain will fall
And never cease to fall,
The skies of grey will shed their tears
And never cease at all,
The sunny days will all have gone
Darkness descending on earth,
And joy will turn to sadness
Crying, 'What was this woman worth.'
And laughter will have turned its head
As myriads will mourn,
And night will embrace everything
And never bring the dawn.

A life so full of caring
Will be in peace at rest
And everyone will realise
They really knew the best.

A selfless, helping angel
That life can rarely bring.
A pleasure everlasting
That made the world to sing.
A joy to love, a joy to know,
All sweetness and all light,
Who lived a life of principle
Divorcing wrong from right,
And lived her life with dignity
Despite the endless pain
Until the tears of sadness
That brought the falling rain.
If I should lose you, the rain will fall
And never cease to fall.

Tony Sheldon

MILLENNIUM'S BUG

I am sure the old millennium's bug
Was in my bed last night
For first I felt a little itch
Then I felt a bite
I showed it to my mother
This blooming great big bump
But all she said was there-there dear
It is only a little heat lump
But still I wasn't satisfied
How can it be I really cried
You can't get heat lumps in wintertime
I told this dear mother of mine
We searched my bed pulled back the sheet
Shook the blankets quite a treat
Out he fell the millennium's bug
Landed on my bedroom rug
We captured him without a doubt
Picked him up and threw him out
I told my mother there and then
To never feed me tripe again
I know a heat lump from a bite
'Twas a millennium's bug who bit me last night
She called me Lady Knowall
Which came as no surprise
'Twas then I told her there and then
Please do not tell me lies.

Eleanor Dunn

ONE HUNDRED

'Twas Grandma's birthday, we all came to see her,
Mum and Dad, my brother and sister.
My aunts and uncles with presents galore,
The room was crowded right up to the door.
She sat in her chair, the great matriarch,
Outside they were all having trouble to park.
Photographers, media, all came to see,
This grand old lady as sweet as can be.
She had so many cards, the best you could glean,
Was the one she received from Her Majesty The Queen.

Renée Honeywell